COZYISMS . . .

THE ART OF PAYING ATTENTION

(THE FIRST RULE IN LIFE)

COZY STONE

The Art of Paying Attention, Book I, offers a unique perspective of the power of words and wisdom – and how TO PAY ATTENTION TO what we see, hear, and experience. These pages were created to *simply* inspire awareness in our everyday lives ... to lift spirits and to motivate all who know better. You will hear yourself saying "ummmmmmmmm" throughout the entire book. You will hear yourself saying, "She's so right!"

The fact is, I see words in action. They appear as "visual jumping beans" both inside my head and ... out they come through my mouth!

The Artist in this book will reveal some of the Jumping Beans in HIS head through HIS visual masterpieces. You will revel in the intricate pieces. They, too, will force you to pay attention.

The relationship of thought-provoking text and the wondrous images will embrace, enhance and evoke feelings of splendor. We are confident you will enjoy both perspectives!

For all readers who have paid attention while reading this book, please accept my heartfelt gratitude.

ISBN: 978-0-578-65948-0

This book is dedicated to the wonderful women in my life who believed in me from our first eye-to-eye; and, who taught *me* to always pay attention ...

Lydia Giles, my mom

Blanche Jordan, my cousin

Libby Bleaman, the best high school teacher and friend any student could wish for,

Together they created this forever student of life.

You can NOT be my God ... But you CAN be my ange

If you don't get over it … I will

If it doesn't feel good ... don't do it

I love me enough … for the both of us

No relationship starts off bad ... so at the end of it, focus on the beginning

That man is so fine … I just need 45 minutes and 30 seconds with him

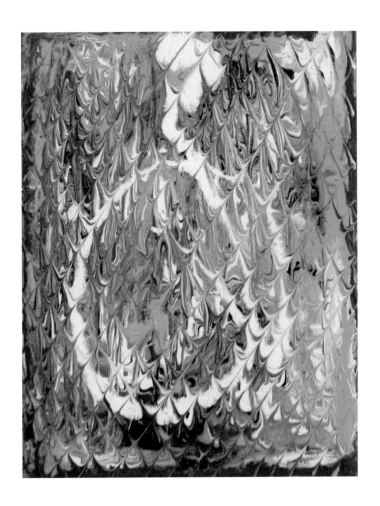

Racism ... What a Colorful Shame

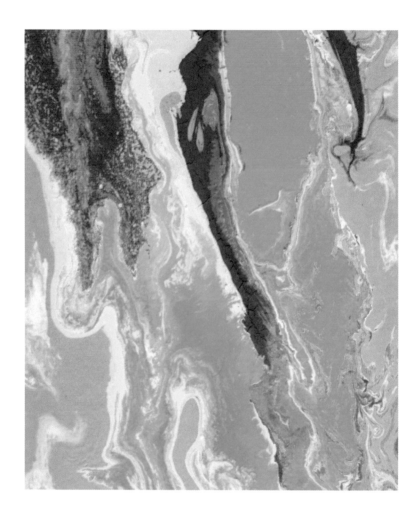

If you're around folks whose feelings you cannot hurt ... be afraid -- be very afraid

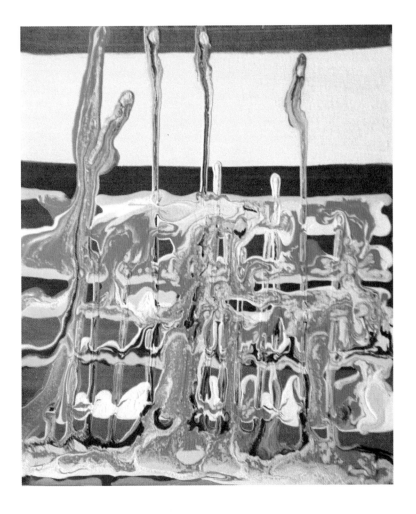

Tell me all you want … show me all you've got

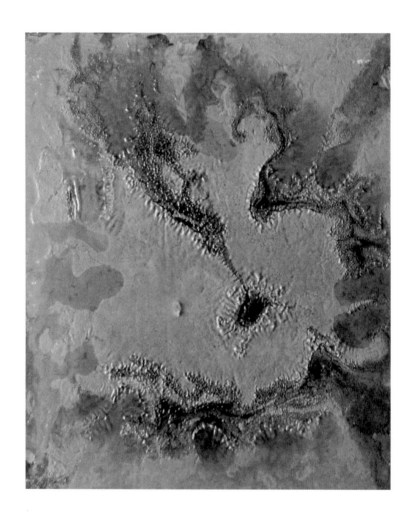

If you can teach them how to pee-pee on the paper ... they won't poo poo on the carpet

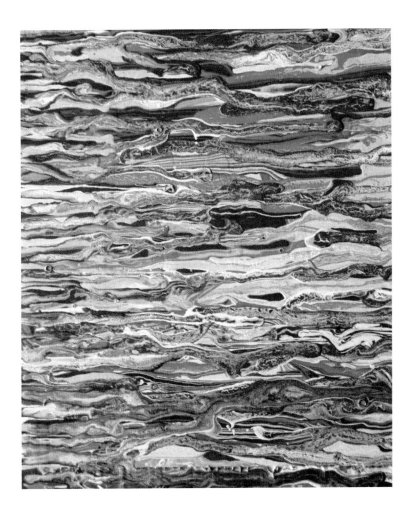

Inactivity is tiresome

For many, it is easier to find themselves ... after being lost

First time shame on you … Second Time shame on you … Third time shame on you

First rule in life ... pay attention

When I die, my soul I take ... it was never for sale

There is no benefit ... of doubt

Page 16

You are obviously taking me personally ... and I don't even know you

Don't waste your time … with those who don't
deserve you

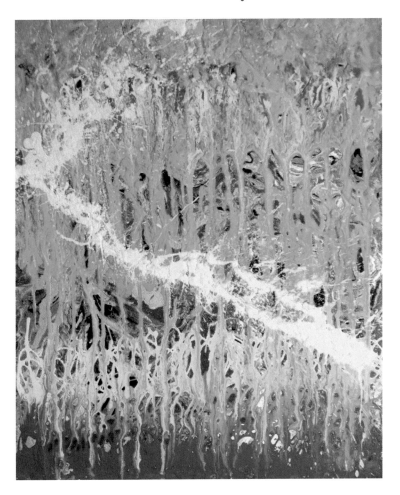

If you don't care ... why should I?

Page 19

Divorce courts are built ... for people who settle

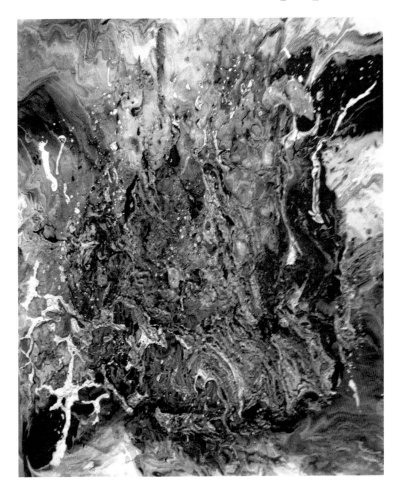

You can be with someone … and be alone

Page 21

The mirror is on the wall … for everybody to see

Just because we share some DNA
… Doesn't mean we have to relate to each other

The heaviest burden to mankind … is always
having to be a man

If all men (persons) are created equal … why isn't equal good enough?

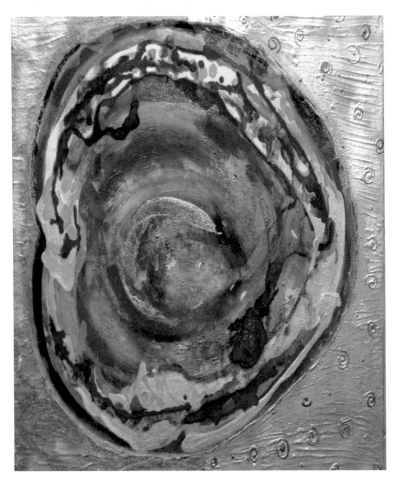

If you do not like your life … why would you put it
on someone else?

Why should your good time … cause a bad time for others?

If the shoe doesn't fit … don't get a bunion trying to put it on

Do you realize you cannot give … what you do not have?

Age: It has a way of allowing pure common sense … to override immaturity

What you wanted from your parents yesterday ...
are your needs from others today

Page 31

The entire time you've been looking for the rose garden
… you've been ignoring the petals under your feet

At this point in your life, you've already f**ked everybody you didn't give a f**k about

I don't know what's wrong … But I know it's not
right

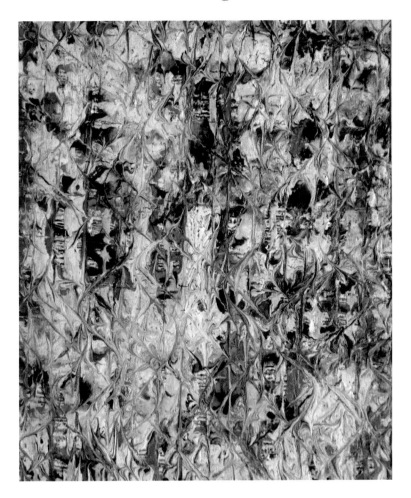

Cozy Stone, Author

Cozy Stone's careers spans from professional executive sales with fortune 500 companies, to comedian, to one of the first personal trainers in the United States, to motivational speaker. Today, she is an entrepreneur in the HumorVational speaking field giving her love and attention to middle school students. She is also available to speak at corporate functions. Visit: www.amazon.com/cozyisms.

Cozy has experienced success in all of her endeavors. Cozy practices what she preaches. In her spare time, she loves to workout, read, enjoy movies, and laugh a lot with family and friends. Cozy presently lives in Las Vegas, Nevada.

Pradeep Gupta, Artist

Pradeep Gupta is a New York based and self-trained artist of Indian origin. He paints in all kind of mediums. His preferred tools of painting are everything under the sky except brushes. His paintings are totally non-conventional and follow no specific school of thought.

Pradeep is a strong follower of peace and humanity. All of his work is inspired from his own life experiences and the way he looks at the world. His paintings seem to be talking to his viewers in their own language. They are bold, bright and stark.

His works can be found in private living rooms of art lovers around the globe.

All of his work in this book can be purchased at www.fineartsamerica.com. More of his work can be viewed and purchased at www.pgartweebly.com.

Made in the USA
Las Vegas, NV
12 November 2020